OPPRESSION

OPPRESSION

poems by
Judith Skillman

SHANTI ARTS PUBLISHING
BRUNSWICK, MAINE

in memory of my mother, Dr. Bernice Bloom Kastner

May 4, 1931 – May 31, 2025

Other Titles by Judith Skillman

AHADADA BOOKS
Prisoner of the Swifts

BLUE BEGONIA PRESS
Beethoven and the Birds
Storm

BREITENBUSH BOOKS
Worship of the Visible Spectrum

ČERVENÁ BARVA PRESS
The White Cypress

DEERBROOK EDITIONS
Came Home to Winter
Kafka's Shadow
Subterranean Address

DREAM HORSE PRESS
The Never
The Phoenix: New and Selected Poems

FLOATING BRIDGE PRESS
Oscar the Misanthropist

GOLDFISH PRESS
(with Jocelyn Skillman)
In Our Resemblance
To Take Us All Home
The Nostalgia of Water

LUMMOX PRESS
Broken Lines—The Art & Craft of Poetry

PLEASURE BOAT STUDIO
House of Burnt Offerings

SHANTI ARTS PUBLISHING
A Landscaped Garden for the Addict
The Truth About Our American Births

SILVERFISH REVIEW
Circe's Island
Heat Lightning: New and Selected Poems
Red Town

Contents

Every Nerve ∾⊙∾

Contagious Spring ∾⊙∾

Acknowledgments

Thanks to the editors of the following journals in which these poems first appeared, some in different versions:

Arkansas Review: "Grift"

Belletrist: "Above Hades"

Bez & Co: "Letter to My Comrades in the Arts"

Blue Unicorn: "In the Garden"

Bracken: "Skittish Horse" and "I See How It Happened"

Cimarron Review: "A Wolf in Her Violin"

Cirque: "Noble Ancestors"; "Penelope Weaves Forsythia"; and "Tenderness for the Old"

Cold Signal: "The Asters" and "Long Hours of Illness"

Commonweal: "A Journey Down the Spree"; "Oppression"; "Snow Globe"; and "The Time to Ask Questions Has Passed"

LA Review of Los Angeles: "Finding Winnipeg"

Literary Hatchet: "Arguments of the Dead"

Narrative Northeast: "Address to My Phantom Limb"; "Bisques"; and "In the benign indifference"

North American Review: "Diaspora" and "Quotidian"

Nifty Lit: "Always Gardening" and "Hostile Planet, Do You Care for Us"

Power of the Feminine: "Two of Every"

Quilliad: "Subsistence"

Second Coming (Indolent Books): "My Fear"

Sunlight Press: "Reflex"

Swanannoa Review: "Penelope's Address"

Switchback (University San Francisco): "It Is Not Easy with the Pelicans"

Tar River Poetry: "Insomnia's Twin"

The Ending Hasn't Happened Yet (Sable Books): "Fibromyalgia: Maledictions for Morning"

Vineyard Literary Magazine: "Thermometer"

•

"Diaspora" appeared in *Subterranean Address: New & Selected Poems* (Deerbrook Editions, 2023)

•

Thanks to my friends and colleagues: Christianne Balk, Irene Bloom, Janée J. Baugher, Tina Kelley, Mary Kollar, Susan Lane, Linera Lucas, Kurt Olsson, Anne Pitkin, Diane Ray, Joannie Stangeland, Mary Ellen Talley, and Lillo Way.

My gratitude to John Sibley Williams for his editorial support.

Littleoldman

Littleoldman sits around counting eggs.
Every time he counts, one egg is lost.
My friends, don't show him your gold.

—Edith Södergran

For Darkness

Two of Every

I am making the same
dress twice.
This dress wants
for nothing.
It has a bodice,
and straps in front,
straps in back.
In one dress the straps
are white. In the second
they are pink.
I am cutting a pattern
for her and for you.
You'll wear the dress
to temple with a hat.
Which one? I am sewing
with thread, the hand
of calico. One day
you'll understand
why I left Quebec,
wandered a hallway
deserted between classes.
Why I live this way
in doubt and dresses.
I make do with making
rather than being,
use soap often,
the harder, the better.
One day you too
will stand in a stiff dress
under a canopy
and be given away to marriage.

Above Hades

She plays with the owls
and the golden dog.
I picture a painterly light
and no more sickness.
She waves away my longing
with just her laughter.
I remember a curtain
of hair through sirens,
I steep tea with cut lemons
and ginger root
to stave off the sickness
of these dark months.
We are parted from flesh and water,
we who learned to smile,
walk, talk, swim. Taste my cries,
crusts of dried foam.
I am Demeter, that gull
whose black eye fastens
on a necklace of shells,
the abalone she wears on her collarbone
long into summer.

Remnant

What's left—a scrap
of memory,
the paisley linen
I made into next
day's miniskirt.
Hand-sewing
the hem before bed,
listening under
sheets, transistor radio
tuned to *Motown*, hair
wet in foam rollers.
And bullies, those girls
who threatened
to take me out back
and beat me with chains.
What remains—bolts
of cloth on Mother's
dining room table
and she too busy
to realize the least
of my problems
was being left-handed.

Valance

For autumn, the women take down
these half curtains of mist and lace,

replace them with brocade and velvet.
It is for darkness they do this.

For the cold hours when candles must be lit
and the dead insist in shadows.

Women lift each swag, shake out
a summer's weight of dust motes.

Quartered, all of a piece, these hours passed
with their girls, and laughter over trifles.

Abandoned by their husbands to small mansions,
women rag fingerfuls of gray dust.

Yellow dog, what are you hunting?
Red-headed daughter, where bound?

Quotidian

No children to leaven
        conversation, no sun
to lighten these sad grasses
        mowed in straight rows.
The only news the news.
        Listen to the chimes tell
their churched secrets.
        I promise to be your nurse
if you tell me, your arm at an angle,
        how a bone heals
stronger than its break.
        When dinner's over,
our hunger sated
        by faux bourbon sauce over chicken
and broccoli noodled
        with ricotta and garlic
outside in the dark
    something will walk beneath
an umbrella. Flashlight,
        dog, no person.
Just dog and light circling one another
        like bicycle pedals.

Grift

Whoever has stood looking out
at the Mississippi River
mulling over its waves,
a great brown tragedy,
will know she is close
to the place where her child
first noticed her wearing a veil.

A fine-gage gauze, sculpted
to her face. At times the child
came to her mother with a question.
The answer drawn as if pulled
from a well, for the child
born with one kidney, ureter bulging
like a mandarin orange into the bladder.

Mother in a sailor collar, a silk dress.
How could the child know
how to pierce an armor so hard
it took the shade of a quip?
The child found herself a language
and a hideout, where wild currant grew
beside a chain link fence.

So far in the story, no dog.
Nothing shattered or broken,
only the toyed-with feeling
of not being heard or seen.
A house becomes registered—historic—
years before an infant is born.
Pity for the girl come
to such a home. Mercy and pity,
and all the waters of the world
flooded with nightmares.

The Asters

Remind me of my father's stars,
        purple-blue,
        though he's been gone these twenty-five years.
                I'd like to ride his promise
                        of a super nova,
to blend with sky,
                be the young star
        held by power, my fear
                quieted by a man
        in whose presence
                        fireballs greened days,
meteors seared nights. Asters in October
        remind me to shimmy
                in search of one good dream.

Penelope Weaves Forsythia

This my wand of yellow,
hint of olive,
myth of three more snows.

This my shattering—to come up
from under. There the owls
plied me with shades,

eye-glinting odalisques set
in trees growing downward, roots
of a body that was mine

back then, before aging.
This my dowry, water
sparkling for hunting and rutting,

a dance I sit and watch,
my long gown gathered and sewn
by green veined hands.

Amphora Preserved in Liquid

This one was made of glass.
She buried it in his tomb
along with the hair pin
he made for her, also glass.

Her hair wavy, thick to her waist.
Color of both sun and moon,
wound into a bun,
she'd stuck that single pin in

a thousand times
before they cut her hair off
for mourning
and sold it at market.

The two-handled jar
beside his feet held oil
for the lamp near their bed.
She saw no reason to light

the lamp after his death.
Their dinnerware—glass
as well. Bowls and plates correct,
edges squared off

like good citizens, even the light
thin and perfect where it entered
the rim of a plate, collected
at the bottom of a cup

to resemble green wine.
It was he who went
empty-eyed to the tomb to wait.
She placed everything he needed

to be comfortable, even rich,
in his next life.
If she kept anything to herself
it might have been

that in her afterlife
she hoped for a different husband,
one less calculated in matters
of the heart.

Thermometer

When mercury sped in silver balls
across the linoleum floor, when father
warned us not to breathe it,
when the glass shattered, it was because
we were sick. Because we were sick
we would get worse, mercury a poison
that rolled and skittered, made a mess
had to be carefully cleaned up,
him squatting over its fumes, using
an eyedropper to suck glistening beads
into one glob he'd dispose of,
leaving glass splinters to be swept up
by mother. We'd let what measured
how sick we were, an instrument
of great importance, break, and we'd done this
after being told *under your tongue,*
close your mouth, wait three minutes. Bad air
took root in the house. Sweats and chills
alternated until after midnight
when one or the other of us would fall
asleep in the full-size. Irish twins marooned
just high enough above the water line
to yawn before drowning.

Silver Lining

You find it resides with much fervor
in an old winter coat,
one of many stored
inside garment bags,
mothball moons gathered the bottom.
One grandmother
stood toothless as she spat
on your head
and welcomed you into a kitchen
full of unleavened crumbs
and poppy seeds.
The other Bubbe
sat with blued hair
and an inhaler, asked you
if you wanted a cough drop,
a peppermint, or a story
of Liverpool during the bombing.
You find buttercream icing
in a suitcase purse,
mohair sweaters that don't itch.
The uncles—even Julio
with his Latin rages—
gone to hell. The aunts
schmoozing color TV,
waltzing nude beneath housedresses
and smoking jackets.

Penelope's Address

From my table I watch blue jays disappear
into full skirted trees at the back of the acre.

Who cares for red-winged hawk or umber squirrel
to take my eyes from loom to sky to eye level.

Like a statue, my ivory hands benign
as myth, my task *ennui*. Lift another skein

from its wooden hook, imagine him alive,
returning home. An oaken door can swing, sieve

these others in to woo the would-be widow
I am not. They make a queue, and how

beautiful I am to be wanted this way.
A *je ne sais quoi* scents yarns I've dyed.

Am I young or old or in between?
Why cry like the siren's islands all sewn

together in the ocean he drank—no swallowed—
without a thought for salt. If he's poisoned

so much the better. He lied about his wish.
I fasten loops, my starfish heart awash

in dreams of suns, moons and happiness.
Is solitude an emblem equal to its fantasies?

Another Childhood

Trees turn black, first bat comes
for a lawn chair, grazing its high back.
A stick flies toward heaven to attract
the next bat, a father's voice calls. Mother
stands on her porch. Leaves lift & settle.
A hot one, they say, & turn sprinklers on.
Droplets spatter halters, arms & legs.
We skip rope, roller skate, climb trees
until the sun heads red-angry to bed.
September stands like a word inscribed
in cedar chips. Hares & squirrels watch us.
We're worse than bad. The whole lot
empty until afternoon, after
we do arithmetic, vocab, escape
the fluorescent prison where we learn
to be alike, when in fact none of us know
what little time we have. Susan least of all,
Stephen with his arm in a cast, Ellen
whose mother died when she was five.

Hard-Wired

Noble Ancestors

You took to the ocean
wearing shabby clothes, holding gutturals,
herded from home by air raids.
The younger son hidden
in a basement, the Anne Frank in her attic
writing to the person her diary became.
What right have I to ask
when you lie all these years underground
without a song to memorialize
the terror of hiding a circumcised
penis, the fear of losing a sister
to the camps? Conjure once more
that laughter ringing from Quebec houses
into the night with its stars and fires,
put your cool hands on my feverish forehead
and wrap me in crochet.
Forgive your children's children
who came after the great wars
to dip their s-shaped fingers
into your drawers,
to read letters telling where the pawn
moves on its board above *Zaydee's* fridge,
and how many *knits and purls*
it takes to make a cabled sweater.

Diaspora

The reed hills take the brunt
        of wailing flung from wind,
                and, where an arm reaches up
from the ground,

beneath mulch and dirt
        shoveled in, only the exposed root
                of a plane tree, elbow-bent and knotted,
hints at the body below.

Time goes by unaccounted, seasons
        take and take. Thistles and scotch broom,
                a few transplanted bouquets
of rosemary, trapped in hollows,

bend and mourn their once green-tipped
        scent. An oboe of bone, a bit of wire—
                concertina, leftover from the other war,
or the one after.

Come to the empty bowl
        your head covered as if you
                are a woman flying like Lot's wife
up a steep path. Others will follow.

Come to the music of ghost notes,
        the body of migrating birds
                searching as one bird, southward
in the throes of dispersion.

I See How It Happened

They were tired of watching robins
in a winter of more than three months,
they'd given up trying to make from chicken thighs
a feast to outlast their vague hunger.
The newspapers could be mistaken
for something else since afternoons
paraded in used clothes, worn record grooves
held the sound of jazz.
Sun shone through spattered panes.
Each house stood silent as usual.
No stone lions guarded splintered porches.
A grand fatigue (or was it malaise?)
visited their kitchens. Bread cost twice
what it had a week ago. Mother
could not venture out due to black toe.
The fatigue of German whispers, rumors—
no details, only fragments, and how
could anything quite so bad come to pass?
No, simply, the cheeses were too soft,
habits too strong to break away from
in the sudden swiftness that took them
to camps in the countryside. There,
coaxed by a bar of soap, they
went naked to shower beneath faucets of gas.

A Journey Down the Spree

The German countryside
does not lament.
It keeps an arbor of green
for those who watch
from a yacht
at center of the river
young girls
hanging laundry on lines
and cheese draining whey
through a net bag.
Houses where the Resistance
entered by stone steps
into damp rooms with wet walls.
We pose as if nothing happened
except *sturm und drang*.
Those taken hostage
in their pajamas
merely agreed to board trains
and sit in shit-filled straw.
They were not fed caviar, remember?

Tenderness for the Old

The way they stepped aside for me,
a child, who judged their lurid furs
fastened about widening bodies.
Every hair colored and sprayed in place
for Auntie Lil, in stark contrast

to Uncle Hi's bald head.
Auntie Bess, who boogie woogie'd
the bared teeth of a piano
sandwiched between dusty Victrola
and vase of dead flowers.

Even the old country, its stories
to which I rolled my eyes,
collapsed in laughter with my sister,
our hysteria unalloyed
by parents who begged us to sleep.

Perhaps worst of all my sins—
trying to escape the grasp of Bubbe
when she grabbed my head
and spat on it to bless me
and keep me from harm.

The Cheek Pinchers

How you've grown—
        how big you are
they say over and again
        as you remain the same,
hard-wired to the past,
        its torturous aunts
and huge grandmothers
        poised like bats in the sky.
Dark figures who want
        to touch sensuous flesh.
You hear a breeze
        through black oaks
in the greenbelt, feel grass
        beneath bare feet.
It's always you in short shorts
        and this is the place
where they gather.

Arguments of the Dead

He says, red-faced
>   *I want to order*

>   *the eggrolls*

She asserts
>   in low tones

>   *We'll have spare ribs*

I squirm in my pedal pushers

>   in a red sticky booth

>   wait for the fortune cookie

>   finally in the back seat
of the Buick
>   unbelted

>   no more than an eavesdropper
on their ongoing *mishigas*

>   gas chambers

>   refugees

His mother a useless prodigy

>   Her mother an orphan

>   their destiny two bad stars

                                    He says, *Look, Venus*
I see

              black trees

                            dirty snow from the plow

          feel lumps under my butt

                                  stuffing of an old taxi

coming apart

            He drives

                            his foot goads the brake pedal

I finger the wrapper in my pocket
                      a string of words

                      He who throws mud loses ground

Chickweed

Ragged, greedy, pliant, easy.
She wore hand-me-downs like her sisters.
Madras and mohair marked her *other*.
Her lack of knowledge about Jesus—when'd
she heard Him praised or prayed to? Only
screamed and cursed if father hit
his fingers with the hammer.
We named her after the pink family.
The chickens took what they wanted,
dragging petals in their beaks. All that shit
and us to clean it. Now we're thinking
how to save what's left of the world.
Her buck-toothed laughter goes on girlish,
infectious in its spread.

Mother's Soap Bar

Never full like the moon or bright as the sun.
An oval disc, a flat zero sat on her
plastic pronged soap holder, getting smaller
until nothing reigned in the bathroom.

Enough for her, though, born in a ghetto.
There, instead of lamb for the seder, they ate
a chicken thigh and murmured over the bone
asking questions God would never answer.

Not Dove or Ivory, rather a no-name
generic kind—*because who can tell the difference?*
she'd say, disparaging those who spent
on a brand when she, simply by rubbing

two pennies together, could make
soups and stews where the rare piece of meat
is tender as a carrot. Half a cabbage
seared in hot oil with onion summoned Poland.

I turn from my upper-middle class room
to meet her in a harsh winter.
Wearing the coat made
by her father the cutter

she walks beside snow plowed in drifts
along Montreal streets. The man in the meme
makes his grab. Mother screams so loud
she slips from his grasp.

In the benign indifference

of the universe, some remnant
of prayer shawl, Kippah, candle.
Vestment, nun's habit, incense.

The moon can eclipse the sun, the moon's red

and the red beads around grandmother's neck
prefer superstition over His risen
body. Did He speak of revolt, defiance,
and passion? What's a four-day-old lamb good for

if not to slaughter and bloody our door frames?

The angel of death comes at midnight.
Camus' stranger shoots the Arab once for death.
Four more times for no reason at all.

Finding Winnipeg

I see my father in slow motion,
a slight figure
playing hockey in a threadbare coat.
Thinner than his two older brothers
who wear their weight warm.

He, my father, first one born
far from Munich,
crossed an ocean in his Ma's belly.
Heard, in utero, retching
in a tiny hold

crowded with other emigrants.
In the tabula rasa
of newly fallen snow
tracks of weasel the opportunist
and prints of fox, his cunning familiar.

Long Hours

Reflex

White noise from the freeway,
white skies of winter,
and, in the body—
where blood once circulated
from the heart
to the tips of fingers
and toes—in the spine
a pinched nerve.

You picture flattened discs
knotted together—you
the once supple gymnast,
the dancer singled out in class
for pointed toes
sweeping a suspended
hardwood floor. You wore
black, held the pose
of string pulled through
neck to head as your youth
arched and swayed.

That back and forth becomes
a cramp in the hip
as the pendulum swings
between your wedding day
and the embalmer
who will dress you
in plain cotton, pull a thin covering
over those questions
whose answers no longer startle
or require.

Long Hours of Illness

I have spent alone, listening
to the spring birds sing and talk
to one another. Trees stand
in the great wood beyond
the window. White filigree
for the cherry, pink for the plum,
and for me merely the blouse
of a peasant who tills her troughs
hoping to find sustenance
in glacial till, to drink afresh
from irrigation channels long gone,
mired in drought.

Address to My Phantom Limb

Close if you will, fist I never knew.
Epitomize grief to a widow
or the sadness of any weekday, and also, Sunday rites
reserved for others—the fasting, the confession.

Ritual depends upon the hand to take in or push away.
Punch the face you lie next to in sensorial science,
if only in representation. Symbolize something.
Isn't that what the mind

does best? Become more than this missing
all I didn't do when I had you hanging from my arm.
Press the center of each note sung by gut strings
against an ebony fingerboard.

Hold the natural hairbrush, stroke color and texture,
compose works as spurious as hogweed
found each August at the back of the acre.
Become horticulture's dreaded cartwheel flower.

Surely you are capable of imitation.
Tighten and release, find the light, lean into noon.
Open fully (even short a pinky)—
release ten thousand toxic seeds.

Let papery skin stretched tight from phalanx to phalanx
dry to a crisp before flipping the bird
to each pursuit I followed
with the passion of one addicted to perfection.

Limbo

It could be the stomach of the whale,
or the white skies of June,
any sick feeling in the gut—
this waiting, scratching off squares
on a calendar page.
It might be a jail cell
with a toilet and cot, the guard
walking past, his gun holstered,
other inmates cursing,
yowling, screaming like cats.
The whale's nowhere to be seen,
and Jonah, though he's confessed,
isn't thrown overboard,
doesn't flail green water
nor get swallowed only to be spat out
for his cliché, specious gratitude.

Subsistence

On a farm called *pain* I wake each day
and each day the same call whistles from slits
and clefts in this body given by the Lord
who made every good thing blue as a jay
or black like night. In this place shadows
stalk the nerves, branches lift and fall. Green's
no more than leaves. My board paid,
I stumble down from the garotte, remember
a painting by some German artist who used
his brush as a surgeon. Memory cuts close.
I'm a new keep, my only duty to morning.
After the cash crop of late lunch perhaps a walk
through neighborhoods if not new still never
as old as this my only body.

Spinal Cord Injury

We live with grasses, clouds, and pain.
It is not easy to see us.
We are like hidden pictures,
books shelved in a library
between other books that tell pretty stories.
You don't want to know
and we don't wish to trouble
your days of ease.
Draw out that strawberry acai refresher
all summer long,
gather at parties on neighborhood decks,
sit on wooden benches.
We forgive the ignominy,
the spell of hysterical laughter,
even these petals
falling from cherries
to land softly on your arms
as the earth pulls us further
into its molten core.

Insomnia's Twin

She comes
with knocked-out teeth
to feast on you
when you're fallow,
out of season, off your game.
Is she bad as her sister,
the one who visited
when you were young
after accidents and surgeries?
Yes, worse, rhetorically so,
more dangerous than you
were then yourself—
you you you
in a bar, at a conference,
you back in high school
doing hashish,
skipping classes, whoring.
It's all about her now
and you know no one
with half a heart
could change the mess
she's made
of your pink sateen sheets.

Maledictions for Morning

Each new day
        winds my body
        in its blatant shroud—
light everywhere, a titanium
        background
against which pain plays.

I am too much with myself.
Inside foreshortened muscles,
        the devil's choir
                requires exorcism.

Each new day winds my body
into its stiff canopy—
        an assemblage
                of neural connections
nonsensical as the verbiage
of that unholy god
                who dared
inflict life on the living.

Rays of light
                poke thin-gage wire,
enter baroque-stained glass,
                wreak havoc
on the calla lily sun catcher.

I remain
        soldered to scoliosis,
                sacroiliitis, stenosis.

You Find Penelope's Thread

A skein of yarn, a button,
the clip you wore when your hair,
boar-brushed, resembled a horse's mane.
Today you are washed,
an elder the seamstress approves
for the way you fit a blouse.
Its collar covers folds of flesh.
Buttonholes allow themselves
to be opened
by arthritic fingers.
Where is she, goddess
who weaves grave clothes by day,
rips them out at night?
Would she approve this drawer
into which you place
contents of your former life—
hair root darkener, eye liner, mascara?
Is she loyal to the tenuous motif
of marriage, its ceremony
braided and twined around two bodies?
One stapled to a spot of land.
The other pelagic, patriarchal,
flirting with sirens.

Obsessive Compulsive Disorder

Plum blossoms pink over leather bark
in April, on cool evenings past
the midpoint of a life. This woman
walks the same route as always,

particular in her aversion
to the precious. Hasn't the plum poem
been written and re-written?
What more is there to say regarding

the death of a son, even if he's not
her own? This woman counting rabbits
reaches a certain number, say seven,
a place to hold against the bobcat's

forays from its thicket, a harbor
in which to drop anchor and survey
all that remains undone, in between,
dirty, disorderly, perfumed with words.

It Is Not Easy with the Pelicans

All morning and deep into evening
they bomb turquoise water,
settle on the surface,

pause with a fish in the long blade
of beak, shake out water,
lean their heads back and swallow.

They drive me to the core of dread
and into the belly of the whale,
where Jonah prays to God in his affliction.

The pelicans' circling
returns me to a kitchen in Eastgate,
my body lying in a pool of blood.

Close to shock, did I think then,
shorn from her placenta,
of my newborn's oxygen deprivation?

No, the red snapper answers from its plate,
one cold eye staring up, asking its hostess
to find the plunge memory requires.

Snow Globe

How many snowflakes fall on this house
with the red roof. A deer comes to graze.
Washed in umber, white-tailed, it nuzzles
drift-fixed wands of blackberry, pulls stems
frothed with inch-thick hoarfrost. Icicles bloom
from failing gutters. If you peer close
a woman wanders from room to room,
glaze-eyed, looking for her lost romance.

Fixed diagnoses: *hallus rigidus,*
spinal stenosis, sifted by a demiurge.
Listen as she washes minuscule dishes,
China small as atoms. After the urge
to leave home wrests loose of the glass
she sits down alone to watch Christmas.

Every Nerve

Skittish Horse

I shy away from two canoes
resting beside a lily pond.
I only want to return to the barn
and join the one who waits
with liquid eyes.
Men took me from the herd,
made the earth so dangerous,
I have to chew it up,
dirty the metal bit that tells
me where she wants to go—
the girl with leather boots.
Water holds sudden trees
and black mountains.
The touch of pine needles
tickles like so many flies.
How can men in their impudence
understand my sinews?
Each pound one of 1200.
Inside every nerve a whip.

Hostile Planet, Do You Care for Us?

Days and nights, moon and sun,
storm and drought—all these happen
to the body as well. Now in this
seventh decade I have to ask
as if you too were a person
who could feel the metal magnetized,
glowing in your poles. Know
the valley as a depression
where only the cactus rose
grows a little succulence to adorn
a place so dry its only comfort
might be the flatness of the floor.

Era

Low-hanging sun
gone to waste like a fruit
unpicked, the sorry story
of war everywhere,
and fires south and east.

When will it heal,
our star once lucky
now gone sour?
Sun my father studied
with his spectroscope,

his penciled decimals scrawled
like insects
across yellow legal paper
to twenty places. I must
have been far younger.

All little triangles—
the pubis, the eaves
full of spiders. I believe
Alice the neighbor (she's
95): You can taste it.

Flowering Plum

Tree with no fruit, I salute you.
This spring may petals
rest a bit longer
before they fall like confetti
to line curbs and cover lawns
in a snowfall so warm
it feels like a dream.

Tree with knotted elbows
and scarred bark,
let me anthropomorphize you
for once, and don't rebuke
a lonely woman
who takes solace in words.
The highest branch

broken by winter becomes
only an arm in a cast.
Do you remember
how I wrote my name on plaster
before leaving algebra and trig?
When it was enough
to contain passion, to flower?

Earth Walks Toward You

Her branches, her wings, her robin
in its *hop hop hop* along deck rails
where black-helmeted birds alight to tear
the moment apart. Is it really already morning?

Mid-afternoon? Evening again?
Needled firs branch and sway. January
dresses you in gray cotton. You
are a hard woman of a girl, too stringent

for the gifts earth brings. Scents of musk
after snowmelt. Heaps of dirt lifted
by moles who carve the underground
with punishing paws and extra thumbs.

Earth walks towards you, her birds and deer,
as you face the cons of staying on, say
your prayers, savor last crops of crabapples,
muscat grapes, and sour cherries.

Oppression

Not the worst part, nightmares.
Not the heat dome
nor the same dun yard
sewn to earth outside the glass slider
with its pinch-pleated burgundy draperies.
Twenty hyenas corner Red the lion
on TV and no one interferes.
Not the producer,
not the one with the camera
nor the British narrator.
The lion a done for.
You can see it in his eyes
as he makes little charges
toward one or the other
while they circle and laugh,
yip, bite his back.

Letter to My Comrades in the Arts

This, then, was our passion, to become Godly
when no other remedy would suffice.
With words, germs, tubes of paint, children
close at hand. With one arm fractured, in a splint
and always more rain or too little rain.
The hammers pounded, freeways widened,
yet our traffic passed unnoticed
as if it was nothing of importance.

Only for us the work went on, seated
uncomfortably far from the center
of a cosmos whose expansion defied
theorists. Nebulae annihilated,
black holes inhaled, our sons died, we mined
our minds for pink Himalayan salt.

In the Garden

Why did we leave our childhoods,
lying on our backs
looking at clouds and their creatures,

staring at the dirt where a flower grew,
petals distinct,
each blade of grass separated

from every other, the white space
between thistle and cat tail?
Why did the meadow recede,

its upside-down daisies like stars
of a constellation knit loosely
to the hill, nestled between

an inch of daylight and the far bank?
Admit we were left with just a blur
and Mars in the sky, planet of war.

Hard-Wired

In the kingdom
     little boys'
         minuscule metal tanks
     and swivel cannons
spit explosions
     enemy chopper
ch ch ch
   lies on its back
     destroyed by flame
can you see the smoke
          ca ca ca ca
     downed jet's plastic cockpit
dumps Lego man
     upside-down-yellow-helmeted
       he shrapnel showers
emerges armed
     b b b b b
     clouds mushroom
the horizon
         pa pa pa pa pa

You Watch

In all seriousness
antics of grown men
throwing a pigskin ball
back and forth.
I watch you watch
and I remember
this is a game.
The real war is outside.
Rain pours from a door
in the sky, tide rises,
covers roads,
drowns houses.
The other war
is when children
move into the quick
where Kalashnikovs held
by mercenaries
fire to kill.
None of these men
are like that.
They are only practicing.

My Fear

Most steadfast companion,
she fishes for fight, flight, fawn.
She wants me to play dead but I am alive.
Dark red her yawn full of teeth.
Native to the country of persecution,
raged at as a child, who could tell
how strong she'd become, her groan
the instrument I play instead of music.
When I capitulate, she grows high
as the Washington Monument. I count
steps to remain sane. When I refuse
to climb she uses the ruse of tyranny
over which I am powerless.
No use side stepping nor acting coy.
She uncoils braids of hair, exposes
the view from her tower in a country
unlike anything either of us ever wanted to see.
Black birds caw at a black-black sky.

Bisques

So many heads thrown on the potter's wheel to be turned, born too early again, unable to see through half-closed eyes. Impossible for the infant to hold its head up. We mothers press the bundle to our breast, feed the suckle instinct, and place the infant with great care against our shoulders, holding its neck in place. Still more are born as if they were pots to be bought by philanthropists. As if they could replace the broken ornaments in razed mosques. We mothers go on holding the head attached to its fleshless body, our palms pressed against this little wick of neck. How could anyone but us know how to feed and change and clothe it? Pulling cotton over the fontanel elicits bouts of screaming, as if the thing were being thrown again into the business of birth. We soothe cries with lullabies. We watch the head sleep on its back without a pillow, see the arms' startle reflex as if falling from a tree to catch a branch. We try not to think of when the skull will be rock-hard, covered in a black hood, dragged by its body into a courtyard to be shot.

Dukkha

Full moon
        stuck between clouds.
The sickness and beauty
        of the moon,
its slippage from the sky
        around father's telescope.
Shining clean, then almost a color,
        finally swallowed by gloom.

An object of suppression,
        the moon, it being lit
by the sun—a yellow dwarf—
        nuclear furnace my father
probed with his spectroscope.
        His trying to make a god
from a star the source
        of all my private agonies.

Homage to Pain

For it tells me I am alive.
For it runs like a gold watch with a new battery.
Its nerves are mine, and I possess
the dressy feathers
of a crow, black from head to talon,
hunchbacked and gnawed at.
If pain is the horizon, lakes
of sulfur and salt bear the names
Alpha and Omega.
Its sharp-needled beak drills my left hip
like a woodpecker.
A two-level lumbar fusion
lifts discs from bone. Pedicle screws give a little limp
to shortened nights.
Praise pain, father of raven,
argument, divinity, foible.

Contagious Spring

Largo

Notes with thick spider bellies,
syrup of winter,
chaste imaginings. The bow
suspended, slowed beyond belief,
ephemeral. There are only
two worlds: in one a horse
with a platinum tail
tears grass. In the other an old woman
sits in a chair, her hair wound
in a bun. You are the go-between.

Pachelbel

A long note a long note and more long notes and then half the length of these notes you play other notes and then you cut those in half so you have eighths and then you cut again as grandmother did with her roll of dough, littler pieces for *die kinder*, sprinkled with cinnamon and sugar. *Dessert music*—you braid the pause to the note, fuse the bow to the string, let the elbow move circles in air, adhere to the script Bach made, a round once known to be played four times in a row because the bridegroom couldn't find the ring and the pianist kept motioning to the players to play. A rustling in the audience because no one notices how many times makes a start or what history is except the marriage takes for a number of years, or it doesn't.

Quiet

I live seven years without children.
The kettle boils its rage away. Suppose
I live in a house under a moon or a stone.
I am old now. No one I need to please
lives with me. Except myself, the one
I tried to avoid with other bodies.
I soothed them at my expense—I own
no defense against those parts with eyes:

self-loathing, self-contempt, sadness, angst.
Left alone as a tot in the care of other
mothers and fathers, yes, the rain affirms,
they could not parent you. No, the furnace
hums, they put up with you but only for
a sum of money. A small girl. A worm.

The Time to Ask Questions Has Passed

Sunset, and the rains are finally over. Stout birds sing.
There are no children here and none visit.
The body is its own quarry. An eye
turns inward, Bach's tender notes fly alone.
A contagious spring reigns over garden.
Crescendo of purple clouds, lime green leaflets,
bawdy weather unsuited to the mood.
Soon, in the dark, the old depression
visits. Leo Tolstoy's Nikita
wakes in the sleigh beneath his master
to live twenty more years as laborer.
To measure with his steps how many straws
it takes to warm a horse in winter.
Three toes gone from each foot, still he walks.

Weeping Cherries

I see two trees standing in eight-gallon buckets
placed before window in the rain. What husband
plants them, I no longer know, our paired life
slipping back to singletons who share a metal roof.
There the woodpecker comes to mate, pecking
chimney to scare the grandchild awake
at dawn. Whites virginal, daubed with blossoms.
Too precious for Persephone, who comes back
in March to tell her mother she is still here. *No,*
I say aloud, *you've been gone too long.*
This is not a prodigal daughter story. Return
to him, the singer in love with metaphysics,
the Greek, the Christian, and eat seeds
placed outside your bedroom door. Go to the mole
who aerates soil, to worms, grubs, those nuts
the squirrel squirreled away last year.

A Wolf in Her Violin

Her teacher told her she had a wolf
inside the *f*-hole, beneath the *G* string, sylph

note crying out when she played, like a cough
on that low string, and she, too young for wolves—

their red fur and strange eyes—believed half-
way through the scales, up and down, the wolf

pulling at meat. Those teeth testing how tough
the ground, how buried a voice might become—safe

enough to walk from low-growing shrubs of
the sanctuary? Why bother listening for the other wolf,

which was gray? She placed one note against itself,
tried to tell where the animal lived. She believed

it was true, the arrangement, and how, when rough
things happened, as they would, which color wolf

might emerge from the Saint-Saens. Or the bluffed
Paganini, Tchaikovsky, other concertos, riffs

blended like hard liquor, and she a girl, or a wolf.
How milk the sly red one for its harsh dark *woof*.

Always Gardening

I plant my fingers against one against the other
    on the ebony board.
                Years pass
      between one practice session and the next.
Here are winter's frozen grounds and arguments.
    Whatever progress was made has been lost.

                In sharps and flats,
the grind of music badly played picks up tempo.
    I begin to remember the reason for pain.
    I hear nothing of your voice speaking in obscenities.
You could say, in a sense,
    the gut is free to be taken
                  from the cat's intestine.

Wayward marigolds sprout near the bridge.
    I notice my sister's blonde-haired blue-eyed
          capture of Mother's attention.
In a duet there are two who understand.
    They give and take the map of these
        and other provinces with equanimity.
Sometimes reddish roots trip my pinky.

           Perhaps I am an elder
    about to become the tilted shin
      of that relative from whom I ran as a child.
My right palm aches from holding brazilwood
    strung with horsehair.

     Heavy with gravity
I remember some sonata I could once play
        by heart.

The cold omnipresent as a god who listens from clear blue sky
        for whatever song he needed in the past.

                        No one cares for icicles.
            They grow from roof to ground
                        like the teeth of a monster
                        or the end
                                of husbandry.

It is for this flecked and frozen collection of atrocities
                        a student must drill deep.
                I lift my third finger
                        from the second.

In the face of this dejected sun lying low
                against trees
I vow once more to let whatever lies beneath a soul trill
                summer, summer, summer.

About the Author

JUDITH SKILLMAN holds a Masters in English Literature from the University of Maryland and has done graduate work in Comparative Literature at the University of Washington. Her "how to," *Broken Lines—The Art & Craft of Poetry* is available from Lummox Press. Work has appeared in *Cimarron Review, Commonweal, Threepenny Review, Zyzzyva*, and other literary journals. Skillman is the recipient of awards from the Academy of American Poets, Artist Trust, Washington State Arts Commission, and Floating Bridge Press. She collaborated on translations of Macedonian poet Jovica Eternijan and French-Belgian poet Anne Marie Derèse. Skillman is also a visual artist who works in oil on board and canvas. Her paintings have been featured in *Artemis, Penn Review, Southern Quill, Thin Air Magazine,* and elsewhere.

www.judithskillman.com

SHANTI ARTS

NATURE ▪ ART ▪ SPIRIT

Please visit us online
to browse our entire book catalog,
including poetry collections and
non-fiction books on nature, healing,
art, and more.

Also take a look at our highly
regarded art and literary journal,
Still Point Arts Quarterly, a feast for
the eyes and the imagination —
available to download for free.

www.shantiarts.com